The Everyday Guide to Primary Geography: Locational Knowledge

Simon Catling
Series Editor: Julia Tanner

Series introduction

Geography is a vitally important component in a rich, broad and balanced primary curriculum. It is a subject that is driven by curiosity about the world, as it is now, and how it might change in the future. It provides the knowledge, understanding and skills necessary to address the great social, economic, environmental and ethical challenges that face humankind in the twenty-first century. It involves not only finding out where places are and what they are like, but also investigating how they have evolved and changed in the past, and how they may develop in the future. It enables pupils to make sense of places they know from first-hand experience, and of the wider world they have yet to explore. It helps pupils to understand their place in the world, and how people and places are linked at every level from local to global. It invites pupils to consider the impact of their actions on the environment, what they value locally and globally, and how they can contribute to the creation of a better future.

As series editor, I hope to inspire you to engage in active 'curriculum making' by providing stimulating ideas that you can adapt, extend or modify to meet the needs and interest of your class and your school's curriculum. All the activities are 'tried and tested', demonstrating how everyday and easily accessible resources, used creatively, can enhance and enrich pupils' geographical learning. Each double page is divided into panels with the key geographical learning opportunities on the left side, supported by downloadable resources available from the web page for this guide.

High-quality geographical work incorporates three key inter-related elements (Figure 1). The first of these is an enquiry approach that involves asking geographical questions and using a range of skills, some specifically geographical, to find the answers. The second is the study of places, such as the local area, town, region, country or, at a global scale, continent or the whole world. The third element involves learning about the physical and/or human and/or environmental geography of the places studied. Combining these different elements can enable pupils to think geographically in authentic learning activities that have real purposes, audiences and outcomes.

Enquiry, geographical skills and fieldwork	• Asking and answering questions • Planning and undertaking geographical enquiries • Communicating the outcome of enquiries • Making and using maps • Using globes, atlases and digital mapping • Fieldwork skills • Using secondary resources such as books, websites and images • Understanding differing points of view
Studying places – place and locational knowledge	• The school grounds and local area • The UK, Europe and the wider world • Localities in the UK, Europe and the wider world • Locational knowledge
Physical, human and environmental geography	**Physical geography** • landscapes, volcanoes, rivers, coasts • the weather, seasons and climate • landscapes, plants and animals **Human geography** • homes, buildings, villages, towns and cities • journeys and the movement of people, goods and ideas • jobs, agriculture, fishing, mining, manufacturing, transport, services • land use and the location of activities **Environmental geography** • change and development • caring for the environment and the planet • sustainability and environmental responsibility

Figure 1: Three key elements in geography.

The series illustrates the amazing scope of geography in the primary curriculum, and the stimulating range of learning approaches it encompasses. It showcases high-quality geographical work contributed by primary classes in the UK and beyond. I hope it will be an inspiration to you to create challenging, exciting and satisfying geographical learning experiences for the pupils you teach. *Julia Tanner*

Resources to accompany this Guide, such as activity sheets, teacher guidance, extra activity ideas and cross-curricular links, are available to download from the Geographical Association website
Go to **www.geography.org.uk/everydayguides**
Click on the button for this Guide and then enter the password **SC19DJ**

Contents

Knowing where's where 4

Developing locational knowledge 6

Enquiring into where's where 8

Locational knowledge resources 10

Saying where, getting there 12

Where's what in school? 14

Where we live 16

World wheres 18

Storyworlds 20

Topically where? 22

Discovering where in atlases 24

Locating places and features 26

My country, my place 28

Exploring time zones 30

Themes, projections and world regions 32

Which places should we know? 34

References and further links 36

Knowing where's where

This guide is about exploring location to stimulate, enliven and enrich geography at key stages 1 and 2. It outlines various approaches and contexts to develop early years and primary pupils' knowledge of where's where in the world – their locational knowledge of places and features in our familiar places and across the world. It also explores some rich possibilities for cross-curricular work through linking geography with other subject areas.

Knowing *where's where* is important for several reasons. It enables pupils to:

- place themselves locally, nationally and globally
- develop their appreciation of distance and scale, nationally, locally and globally
- be curious about their region, country and other places in the world
- know where in the world events occur and how these events affect them
- build up their sense of the planet and their place within it
- develop their awareness of global diversity.

The value of locational knowledge

Locational knowledge (or knowing where's where) is a fundamental aspect of geography. It involves knowing and understanding where and what places and features are as well as why and how they came to be located in a particular place. In order to make use of their locational knowledge on a daily basis, pupils must acquire both directional language and locational language. Geography is where they can develop and apply this language (for more, see 'Acquiring locational knowledge' download – see web links).

In order to get around their local area, or place themselves in the world, pupils also instinctively develop locational knowledge. They do so by creating, retaining and constantly updating (correcting) their own maps from memory (or mental maps) of their home area as well as at regional, country, continental and global scales. From their earliest years, pupils become aware of these scales, and, over time, the scales at which they think about the spatial structure and nature of the world become intermingled.

Local memory maps

Locational knowledge is invaluable to pupils' lives. Knowing their way around their home area, the location and alignments of local streets, where the shops, library and friends' houses are, and the links between them all enable pupils to use their locality to the full. Pupils develop familiarity with places through exploring and experiencing them first-hand. When they encounter new features locally, pupils immediately make links with their prior knowledge of the area. Pupils (and adults) do this naturally, creating their own memory maps of local places and features. It is through geography that pupils extend and deepen their knowledge of what's where and come to understand that the interconnections between places are fundamental to their lives.

National memory maps

However, pupils inhabit a world beyond the local. Gradually, through visiting, reading and hearing about other places, pupils build up locational knowledge and a sense of living within a larger regional and country-based community. Pupils often learn where a place is beforehand (from a member of their family) or on the journey to it (by looking at a road map, accessing the family satnav, or via Google Maps).

Pupils see maps showing places on television news, in newspapers and on the internet. They incorporate this information into their own regional memory map, building a sense of where places are in relation to each other nationally. Through primary geography, pupils can connect their part of the country with other regions.

Global memory maps

At school (and at home) pupils learn where places are in the world. They develop their knowledge of the continents and oceans, and come to understand that our planet is a globe (oblique spheroid), which has many different features. In geography, pupils investigate these features using satellite and aerial images, atlases, world maps and globes. Over time, pupils construct their own global memory map. This helps them remember not only their own place, but also where other places are located in relation to theirs and to each other. In this way, when an event occurs elsewhere in the world, pupils are quickly able to work out whether it is near or distant from their country or continent.

Using this guide

This Guide has been written for classroom teachers, trainee teachers and teaching assistants working in primary schools. It will also be a useful resource and reference for geography co-ordinators or subject leaders, and senior leaders responsible for whole curriculum planning or the quality of teaching and learning. The Guide will be of interest to educators who are excited by holistic and creative approaches, and to those who believe that primary pupils learn best when they are stimulated and motivated by engaging and challenging learning activities.

The aim of this Guide is to encourage the use of locational knowledge in primary geography teaching and learning. Each of the 12 double-page spreads provides brief information about the aspect of locational knowledge developed and outlines an idea for introducing the work. There is a range of geographical activities together with details of the geographical potential developed using that approach. An accompanying web page provides cross-curricular links and resources, including web links where extra material can be accessed. In some instances, the downloadable materials include contributions from practicing teachers.

The ideas offered for using each locational knowledge approach contain suggestions across key stages 1 and 2, and most can be adapted for use with other age ranges.

This Guide is intended to encourage teachers to explore and develop the full potential of locational knowledge as a stimulus for geography-based work. It should also inspire teachers to be adventurous and creative as they experiment with these ideas in their geography teaching.

Developing locational knowledge

Evidence suggests that the extent of pupils' locational knowledge varies between individuals and between countries, with few instances of extensive knowledge of national and global locations. Yet, clearly primary pupils make perfectly good sense of the local area through experience, and are able to learn their way around quite quickly in new localities. Experiential learning that makes connections for and sense to pupils seems most helpful in developing their locational knowledge. Consistently using globes, atlases and world maps helps pupils gain a sense of the wider world; often they become genuinely interested in the places and features mentioned and motivated to find out more.

Mapping their world

Unsurprisingly, perhaps, in their earliest attempt at drawing maps, most 5–7-year-olds include places and features that are important to them personally. Even on maps of the local area, the features tend to be discrete, with no awareness of the connections between them. Often teachers need to ask the pupil to explain how and why they have shown features and places in this way. This age group's national and world map drawings also tend to include real places as separate shapes (e.g. a shape for London shown alongside one for England) and neither shape will be accurate. This indicates that 5–7-year-olds have yet to grasp the idea that places are nested within each other.

At 8–11 years old pupils begin to grasp the relationships between places (i.e. 'nested hierarchies') and start to produce local, regional, national and world maps that show they can make connections between places and features. Nevertheless, at this age, the pupils' ability to show links between places and features will depend on their experiences of using a range of maps, atlases and globes within and beyond the geography classroom.

Throughout their primary years, pupils will build up their locational knowledge by learning the names of places, where they are and what they may be like in a range of ways. Whether it is from travels with family, hearing friends talk about places, seeing something on the television news, their own interests or through school investigations – pupils should be encouraged to explore the local and wider world and their place in it.

Photo © Paula Owens

Good teaching practice

There are many ways to build and extend pupils' locational knowledge. Learning about where places are depends on several practices that benefit pupils' learning.

As their teacher, you can show a genuine interest in and promote noticing where places/features are to help your pupils begin to appreciate what they are. Use examples, illustrations and discussion – all essential in learning about places at all scales.

When pupils investigate the school grounds (or local area or further afield), make sure they have access to large-scale maps, aerial and satellite images, newspapers, the internet and so on. Thus, pupils can identify where places are as well as their proximity to and relationship with other places, and recognise that these locational connections are important.

You should refer to globes, maps and atlases at every opportunity. Encourage your pupils to locate places on globes, maps and in atlases then share their findings with others. Make noticing what is where an everyday activity and ensure pupils can constantly browse atlases, globes and maps alongside other resources.

In early years and reception settings, have softball and inflatable globes in with tactile play resources. Ensure pupils have plenty of opportunities to look at them and talk about what globes show. Use inflatable globes as *aide memoires* throughout the primary years to enhance pupils' learning about the world.

Five-year-olds are able to recognise key features and places on maps of their country, continent and the world, so devote time to talking about what they see. Where appropriate, draw pupils' attention to the symbols, colours, names and numbers used on maps. Older pupils may need help to understand what globes, maps and atlases exclude and see the limitations to using them.

When planning geography and geography-led cross-curricular topics for and with pupils, note any places they name and provide opportunities for pupils to check or find out where they are. Whatever the context or scale, it helps pupils' learning to know about places and their location.

Make the most of cross-curricular opportunities with numeracy, for instance, when pupils learn to use grids and grid references to locate places, map scales and measure distances on maps.

What to learn about locational knowledge

This guide outlines various approaches and contexts to develop early years and primary pupils' locational knowledge of places and features in familiar places and across the world, so what seem to be the key components of locational knowledge? Through their geographical studies primary pupils should use paper and digital local, national and world maps, atlases and globes to develop their knowledge of where is where. To do this they need to become familiar with several important aspects of locational knowledge and geography:

- the features and layout of their school and its grounds, and of the local area and where it is regionally, to develop a sense of local and national space
- their own country and its constituent parts and shape – including the region in which they live, the continent it is in, and its main physical and human geography features, including some key cities, mountains, rivers and lakes, and its main uses of land – to make spatial sense of their home country
- the names of the continents and oceans, and which is where, alongside the names and locations of various significant countries and cities (including some capital cities), rivers, mountains, lakes and islands, and about the locations of environmental regions and biomes, to develop their spatial sense of the world
- the various ways in which maps use dots, lines, shapes and colours to show features, places and areas locally and in countries, continents and the world; to understand how spatial information is represented on maps and to begin to appreciate cartographic language. This includes reading place and feature names and understanding what the numbers on maps mean
- some ways in which people have used spatial constructs to understand and locate features and places in the world: another aspect of cartographic language. The uses of relative and compass directions, the use of grid systems for stating

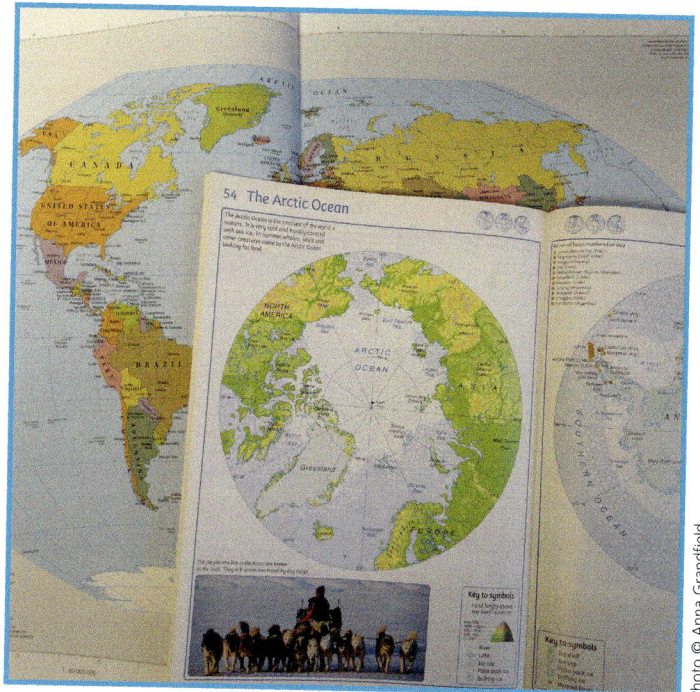

locations, the purpose of latitude and longitude for location, the whereabouts and names of Earth's great circles (Equator, Tropics of Cancer and Capricorn, Arctic and Antarctic Circles), the North and South Poles, the world's time zones (including the Greenwich Meridian and the International Date Line), and the roles of relative and metric scales to show and measure distances and areas

- what the features of the world are, beginning to grasp a rudimentary idea of what a country is, and learning where countries are and what it means when the word 'capital' is mentioned.

Using large- and medium-scale maps and atlas maps is essential for fostering pupils' local, national and world knowledge. In atlases cities, land uses, mountains, rivers and islands as well as countries and major cities may be visually illustrated by feature and aerial and satellite photographs. Differences in scale and the uses of these terms must be discussed: there is little point in pupils knowing words such as 'lake' or 'city' without developing some knowledge and understanding of what they refer to.

Through their use and studies of globes, maps and atlases pupils learn about what these include and exclude, how to use the contents page and index, and how maps and atlases provide locational information. Furthermore, pupils become aware of the limitations of globes, maps and atlases. They can compare what various atlas maps include and discuss why they differ and what they show in common.

Noting what is where is important in developing primary pupils' locational knowledge, but requires context and is best developed within geographical topics, not in isolation.

Enquiring into where's where

Locational knowledge is better developed through geographical enquiries: finding answers during investigations to geographical questions. An enquiry question like 'why is this place significant?' will generate several different answers, whereas locational questions, such as 'where is Afghanistan?' generate precise responses. Thus, an enquiry approach encourages the class to go beyond precise location-based responses and discover why it is useful to know this information, what is important or helpful about it and why it might matter. Geographical questions that focus on 'what is this place like?' will encourage your pupils to think about where somewhere is, the variety and diversity within that place, what happens there and what it may be like to live there.

The framework in Figure 1 outlines the enquiry process. It provides a guide to working from what pupils already know about features and places to what they need to find out, and which resources to access. Figure 1 indicates that investigating 'where is it?' alongside such questions as 'why there?' and 'with what impact?' are integral to every geographical enquiry. Pupils should keep these questions in mind as they follow their enquiry through, thinking about how they record locational information and why this is helpful in the overall study. This leads to the use of appropriate resources to find the necessary information and, perhaps, a consideration of the locational value of the resource. Through working together, reflecting on and evaluating what they study, you and your pupils can discuss the role of locational knowledge and the importance of location in geographical investigations.

Figure 1: An enquiry framework. Source: Owens and Richardson, 2010.

Asking
Use a mix of given and pupils' own questions as a starting point:
What do I already know?
What do I think I know?
What do I want to know?
What vocabulary do I need?

Collaborating
Working together, how will we find out...?
Which are the best questions?
Where will we find answers?
What resources can we use?
How will we do this?

Evaluating
What have we learnt?
How do we know?
Has it changed our thinking? If so, how?
For example, through self- and peer-assessment activities
What new questions do we have?
What next?

Choosing skills, techniques and resources
How will we analyse and present information?
For example:
Data loggers? Video? Stories?
Reports? Graphs? Tables?
Pictures? Drama?

Communicating
What do we do with this knowledge?
Who can we share it with, and how?
For example:
Peer feedback
School website
Class presentations
Assemblies
Parent newsletters
Letters to the local press and MP

Reflecting
What have we found out?
What does it mean?
How does this affect my life?
How do I feel about...?
Do we all share the same point of view?

Central elements:
- Starting knowledge
- Attitudes & values
- Skills
- New & emerging knowledge
- Creativity
- Critical thinking

Managing the learning process

Although the development of pupil's locational knowledge is accretive, it does not necessarily build up in a logical or coherent way in their minds. This is because pupils' range of experiences can be very different given their individual family, social and school contexts. Figure 2 outlines a sequence of opportunities that allow you to help pupils develop their locational knowledge from the local to the global. The overlap of ages in Figure 2 is deliberate, because pupils develop their knowledge of where's where differently. The sequence of activities is designed to enable pupils to study a variety of places using a range of resources while simultaneously developing their local, national and global mental maps.

Initiating locational knowledge (3–4 to 6–7-year-olds)	
Local to regional	**National to world**
• Become familiar with features and locations around the classroom and school grounds. • Use playmat maps to name features, say where they are and what they are next to. • Use everyday vocabulary to talk about places and give and take directions. • Talk about school site on aerial images.	• Play with toy globes and learn that we call our planet Earth (and the world). • Talk about satellite images of Earth. • Use a globe to name and say how land and seas are shown; identify and name continents. • Match cut-out shapes of continents to globes and world maps.

Developing locational knowledge (5–6 to 8–9-year-olds)	
Local to regional	**National to world**
• Use correct locational and directional vocabulary to state where features are in the classroom, school and locally; give and follow directions. • Name and state where features are on large-scale maps and aerial images of the school and locality. • Become aware of other localities in the wider region, using appropriate maps. • Begin to use alpha-numeric grid references to locate features on a school or local area map and talk about map scales.	• Be familiar with the shapes and names of continents and seas. • Recognise the shape of their country and name it. • Identify their country on a continental map. • Use a suitable atlas to find and locate specific places. • Relate the key features on atlas maps to globes. • Talk about specific features of the world on satellite images and world maps. • Become familiar with key places nationally (e.g. constituent nations, capital). • Use the four cardinal compass points.

Extending locational knowledge (7–8 to 11–12-year-olds)	
Local to regional	**National to world**
• Use locational and directional vocabulary and language correctly. • Become familiar with local aerial images and different map types and scales. • Identify and describe familiar features, locations and routes on local and regional maps. • Identify features, locations and routes between key places on regional maps. • Give information about regional localities using maps and photos. • Learn to use 4- and 6-figure grid references. • Measure local distances on maps.	• Use globes and atlases to locate places and features. • Be aware of distances between different parts of the world. • Identify similarities and differences between satellite images, globes and atlas maps. • Know where significant countries, cities, islands, rivers and mountains are on a world map. • Use map symbols and keys. • Be aware of what maps do not show. • Know about Earth's tilt and rotation and how it affects day, night and seasons. • Use latitude and longitude and know about time zones. • Use eight compass points • Discuss and compare maps and distances on maps.

Figure 2: A sequence for managing the development of primary pupils' locational knowledge.

Reference

Owens, P. and Richardson, P. (2010) *Geography Plus: Primary teachers' toolkit series*. Sheffield: Geographical Association.

Locational knowledge resources

Make sure locational knowledge resources are available centrally and/or in different classrooms to share as necessary. Access to these resources is essential for all pupils to learn about places.

Globes, maps and atlases

- Softball and inflatable globes
- Solid globes on stands
- Solid hand-held globes
- World and UK wall maps of different sizes and scale
- Maps of each of the continents
- Maps of countries
- Playmat maps and other durable national and world maps
- OS maps of local area/region
- Digital maps at local, national and global scales (e.g. Digimap, Google Earth/Maps, Bing Maps)
- Local area maps
- Large scale plans of classroom, school buildings and grounds
- Topical issues maps (e.g. from television news, weather maps)
- Tourist maps, postcard maps, souvenir maps (e.g. on tea-towels, pottery)
- Photos of maps displayed in local area (e.g. town centre maps on hoardings)
- Board games based on maps of the world and/or of imagined world, jigsaw maps, fabric maps, etc.
- Early years and primary atlases
- Adult reference atlas
- Urban, regional and national road atlases

Ordnance Survey resources

- OS Mastermap – a large-scale OS plan, available digitally through Digimap for Schools, at scales ranging from 1:1000 to 1:10,000
- OS Explorer Series is published at 1:25,000 scale
- OS Landranger Series is published at 1:50,000 scale
- Historic OS maps are available for various years, and scales include 1:1250, 1:2500, 1:10,000, 1:12,500, 1:50,000, and one inch to the mile
- Digimap for Schools, the online mapping service for use in education, provides access to a range of current and historical OS maps, including OS Mastermap, as well as digital versions of the Explorer and Landranger series.

A library of free resources is available (even for those who do not subscribe to Digimap), and many of these can be used with printed maps. This includes maps obtained from free sites – such as the National Library of Scotland website, which offers historical maps as well to explore change over longer periods of time: https://maps.nls.uk

Photo © Bryan Ledgard

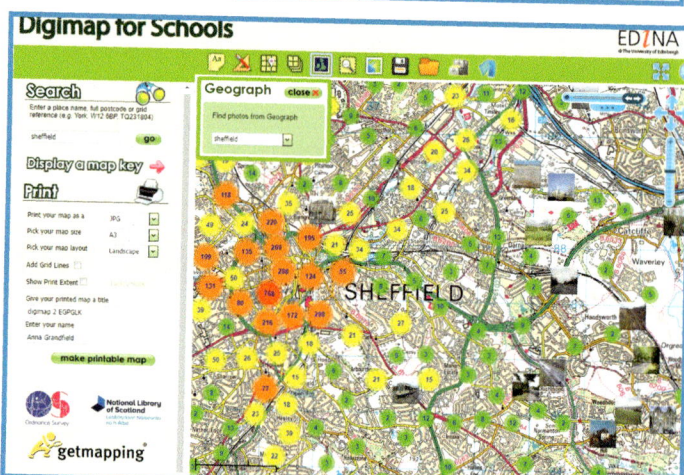

The Meaningful Maps Project (http://meaningfulmaps.org) aims to research children's ideas about locality through maps. On their website you can view hundreds of maps drawn by primary pupils, alongside ideas for why this is so important.

This project offers potential for talking about pupils' own special places and how places are represented on maps.

Other forms of maps and plans are also useful in local-area locational enquiries. These include architects' plans, street maps, road atlases, bus and railway maps, plans of shopping malls or parks, picture maps in tourist brochures, postcards maps, and maps in newspaper advertisements and on websites. Digital maps on Google Earth, Google Maps and other online packages and websites enable pupils to manipulate and experiment with maps, and to view satellite images and aerial photos of the school and local area.

Online images, audio/video and webcams

- Aerial images of the school grounds and local area (e.g. from Google Images/Earth)
- Satellite images of regions and whole Earth
- Extracts from audio and video material
- Online webcams

All online searches (including using Google Images for images, Google Video or YouTube for videos, or Google for webcams) will result in a plethora of results. You will find that some images, audio/video extracts and webcams are unsuitable or inappropriate for pupil use (because they carry tourist information, advertising and other material). It is best practice to vet all online resources before deciding whether to use them in the classroom. Before you use webcams in the classroom, establish first whether the content is live or if the images are a few hours or days old. Find webcams that suit your purpose (e.g. ones showing night-time images when pupils are at school).

Online maps and map skills

- Local to global maps: Encarta world maps, Google Earth, Google Maps, Bing Maps, Worldmapper
- Map skills practice: National Geographic map machine, OS Digimap for Schools and OS MapZone
- Map projections and activities: Oxfam Mapping Our World
- Investigating grid references and map symbols: GA online teaching resources
- Artful maps: GA online teaching resources
- *In the Know – Grid references and map symbols*: GA shop
- Geography quiz using atlases: TES teaching resources
- Mini Map Makers: https://minimapmakers.co.uk/

Check map and map skills websites to ensure the material is suitable for the age range you teach and, wherever possible, adapt their suggestions to suit your pupils' needs.

Children's stories aiding locational knowledge

Ahlberg, A. (2014) *Kicking a Ball*. London: Penguin Books.

Ahlberg, A. and Amstutz, A. (1992) *Funnybones: The ghost train*. London: Heinemann.

de Beer, H. (1987) *The Little Polar Bear*. New York, NY: North South Books.

Donaldson, J. and Scheffler, A. (2003) *The Snail and the Whale*. London: Macmillan Children's Books.

Glynne, A. and Senior, T. (2016) *Hamid's Story: A real-life account of his journey from Eritrea*. London: Wayland.

Hollyer, B. (2002) *Wake Up World*. London: Frances Lincoln.

Kim, P. and Sanchez, S. (2014) *Here I Am*. London: Curious Fox.

Readman, J. and Honor Roberts, L. (2006) *George Saves the World by Lunchtime*. London: Random House Children's Books.

Sutton, E. (1978) *My Cat Likes to Hide in Boxes*. London: Puffin Books.

Wainwright, J., Moran, P., Wiltshire, S. and Ecob, S. (2011) *Where's the Meerkat?* London: Michael O'Mara Books.

Walsh, M. (2004) *My World, Your World*. London: Picture Corgi Books.

Saying where, getting there

Pupils use locational and directional vocabulary in the classroom.

Geographical enquiry and skills

- use relative location and directional language
- use and understand geographical vocabulary
- use observational skills in play

Geographical knowledge and understanding

- features of their classroom
- journeys around the classroom
- create 'maps'

Photo © Lowton St Marys

The youngest of pupils can quickly learn where things are in familiar settings, so the focus here should be on applying vocabulary correctly in the classroom. Pointing classroom features out to them or asking a pupil to get something out/put it away facilitates their locational learning. To reinforce their awareness and use of relative directions, mention specific terms (e.g. 'left', 'right') regularly in the context of going to and finding items around the classroom. Model the use of locational and directional information, for instance, saying "Go straight ahead past the big table to the cupboard with the tins of crayons on it. Next to the crayons is the plastic globe. Carry the globe back to where we are here…" gives directions, names and locates features on the route, identifies objects the pupil will know, names the item to be collected and states where to bring it. When they draw maps encourage pupils to correctly name the features they include.

Where in the classroom…?

Sing the 'Left and right song' with them to establish that pupils know their 'left' from 'right' (access a video on YouTube if necessary). Using the locational set of vocabulary cards (downloaded from the EGPG webpage) encourage pupils to use different ways to answer: 'Where in the classroom am I?' and 'Where in the classroom is…?'. Scaffold responses initially – e.g. 'I sit next to Anya, in front of the bookshelf' or 'The globe is on top of the cupboard'. Point out that they use these kinds of descriptions all the time and as they move about the classroom.

To access extra resources from the Everyday Guides web page, see page 2.

Teaching activities

Routes around the classroom

As an opener, you could walk around the classroom describing your route, then stop and ask pupils 'How do you get from the door to your table?' Challenge pairs to walk a familiar route, with one pupil directing the other. They must use the Vocabulary cards (see web page) and mention any features they pass. The second pupil then directs the first back along the route. Once everyone has completed a route, pairs can share their observations.

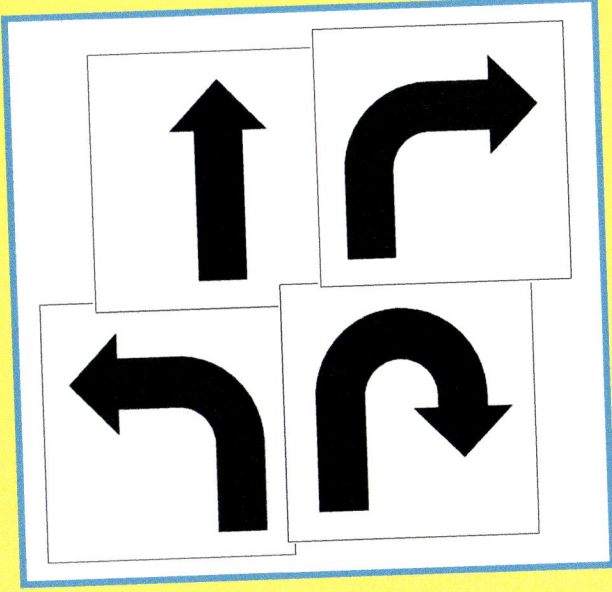

What is it? Where is it?

Give small groups images of different classroom features (one for each group member) and ask them 'What is it? Where is it?'. One pupil from each group must walk to the first feature and back, using the vocabulary cards to describe the route. The second pupil does the same for the second feature, and so on. When they have visited all the features, pupils could give 'What it is, where it is' directions for another group to follow.

Play mat maps

Whenever the opportunity arises, encourage your pupils to look closely at features shown on the classroom play mat map. As they trace routes from one side of the mat to the other using model vehicles and toy people, ensure pupils use locational and directional vocabulary. When pupils 'drive' a model car along the road on the mat, you could ask 'How and why do we make car journeys?' or ask them to describe the car's journey (e.g. 'To get to the shops, do you go straight on or turn left?') Similarly, as they 'walk' toy people around, draw pupils' attention to pedestrian routes by saying, for example, 'people can cross the road here and walk along this path, but they cannot walk over those houses'. When pupils add model buildings to the scene, encourage locational responses by asking 'why there?'.

Arrow maps

Arrow maps are a way of introducing your pupils to practical mapping in the classroom. On a blank sheet of paper, they first mark their location with a cross then draw the feature(s) next to them. They walk round the classroom adding arrows to show when and where they turn and drawing each feature they pass. When familiar with this task, pupils can draw arrow maps with no features and follow each other's arrow maps, reporting on any difficulties and suggesting improvements.

Where's what in school?

Pupils carry out practical mapping activities in school.

Geographical enquiry and skills

- more precise use of locational and directional vocabulary
- fieldwork – use observational skills
- describe locations and routes using own and other maps
- enquiry – ask and answer questions
- map work – using large-scale plans to record and present information

Geographical knowledge and understanding

- features in the school grounds
- identify features, places and routes around school

References

Richardson, P. and Richardson, R. (2016) *Everyday Guide to Primary Geography: Maps*. Sheffield: GA.

To access extra resources from the Everyday Guides web page, see page 2.

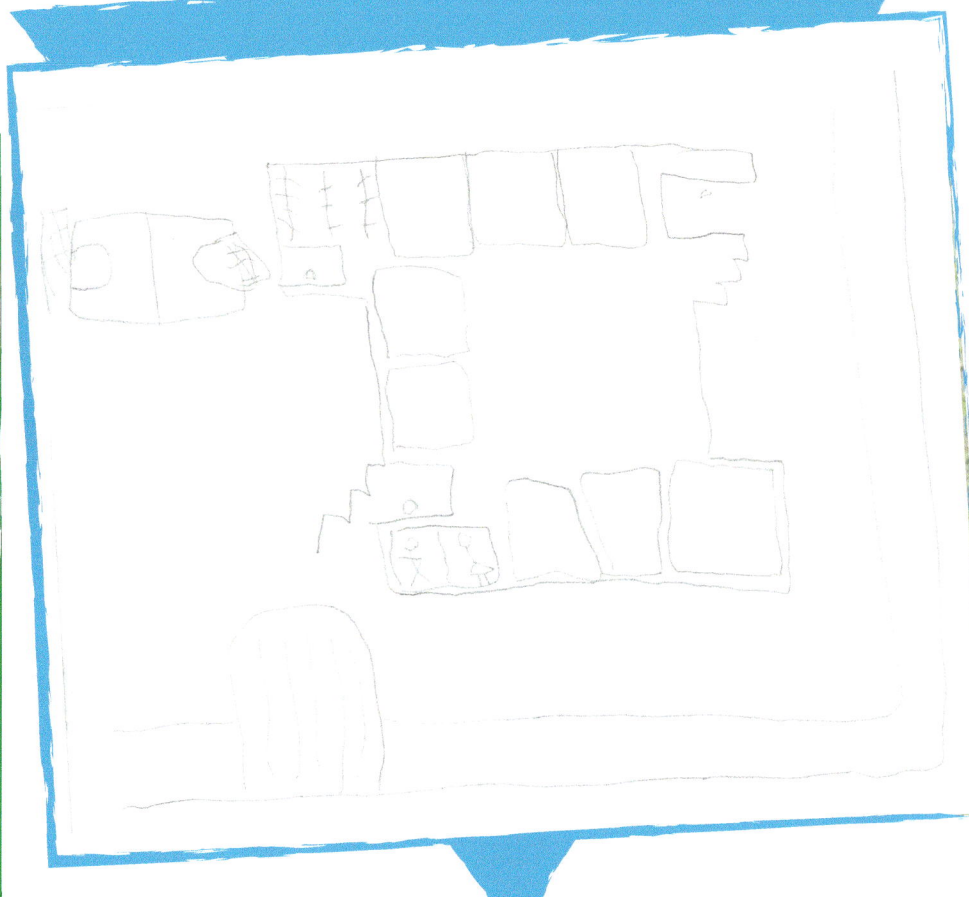

Through direct experience in school – when they carry out tasks and engage in outdoor play with each other – pupils create their own maps from memory of the school buildings and its grounds. Although they may not be aware of it, their memory maps enable pupils to cope with the fact that they cannot see all of the school and its grounds at once. Discuss what they know about the school buildings and grounds (i.e. their locational knowledge of it) and record some of their observations. Pupils carry out a series of increasingly challenging practical mapping activities to explore where's what in the school in more depth, and you can include work on the four cardinal compass points. The activities outlined here are designed to enhance pupils' knowledge of the school's physical and human features and understanding of the spatial relationships between them.

Memory maps of school

Ask individual pupils to draw a map of the school buildings from memory. They should show the location of your classroom and two or three other features of their own choosing. Working in small groups, pupil then draw up a more detailed memory map, discussing and locating their classroom plus the features from the individual maps. Store all pupil and group maps from memory in a safe place for future reference.

Teaching activities

Unlocking what's where

On the interactive whiteboard, display a plan of the school that shows some features as symbols and includes a key. As a class, discuss what the map shows and how. Small groups then identify one missing feature and devise a symbol for it. Using the correct geographical vocabulary (download the Vocabulary cards – see web page), they describe what their symbol shows, say where it should go on the map and add it to the key. Discuss whether the symbols have been located correctly and adjust the plan as necessary then save it. Display the finished plan and provide copies for pupils to compare with (and add annotations to) their memory maps. (See pages 10–11 of Richardson and Richardson, 2016, for more map symbol activities.)

Exploring routes around school

Provide pupils with a detailed map of the school and its grounds. Refer back to the symbols they added to the school building map to refresh pupils' understanding of how to 'read' map symbols and use a key. Go outside and ask your pupils to identify and label the playground features then to mark the routes they use regularly on their maps. Divide the class into small groups and designate them as A/B, C/D... Explain that group A must write instructions (using feature, locational and directional vocabulary – see web page) for a route around their favourite playground features. Group B must follow group A's instructions, marking the route on their maps. Groups then swap tasks. Ask groups: What did you explore? Why? Was the route marked correctly? What changes would make the instructions clearer?

Exchanging maps

In the classroom, pairs of pupils draw and label features on an outline map of the school playground, then exchange maps with another pair and use the maps outdoors. Pairs can suggest changes if needed.

North, south, east, west

Introduce pupils to compass points in the school playground. As a class, first establish which way is north, then work round until pupils have all four cardinal points chalked on the playground around where they stand. Ask individuals 'What can you see when you face north/south/east/west?' Explain that compass points are not like left and right (which change depending on which way they face), so the north side of the school grounds (and the school and local area) is always the north side. Pupils could sketch the view facing each direction, marking the appropriate cardinal point at the top centre of each sheet. You could tape their drawings together at the edges to create an 'All points' hanging display.

Where we live

Photo © Shaun Flannery

Pupils carry out local studies using a range of resources.

Geographical enquiry and skills

- use locational and directional language increasingly precisely
- use observational skills in the school's locality
- describe locations, directions and routes using a map
- enquiry: ask and investigate questions about locations and directions

Geographical knowledge and understanding

- name and describe physical and human features in the local area
- recall and identify features, sites and routes in the local area

References

Richardson, P. and Richardson, T. (2016) *The Everyday Guide to Primary Geography: Maps*. Sheffield: GA.

Google Street View/Maps

To access extra resources from the Everyday Guides web page, see page 2.

There are many different ways to build up pupils' locational knowledge of the area immediately beyond the school gates. Local fieldwork that draws on what pupils already know about the area – i.e. their local mental maps – is a good hook into the topic. Investigating what's where locally should involve pupils in finding their way around, making and using maps, reading stories, checking information on the internet, accessing historical material in the local studies library, studying satellite images and discussing the accuracy of maps in the light of changes to the area. Provide maps that your pupils can relate directly to the environment they are working in and encourage them to talk about what a map shows before using it. For example, to focus pupils' attention on a given area, draw or source a picture map of a local street, market square or park. You can also declutter published maps (e.g. remove unwanted labels) so that pupils see only what is pertinent to the task.

Find local features

Hand out a satellite (or vertical aerial) image of the school and its neighbourhood to pairs of pupils. Pupils take turns to identify and describe a feature on the image for their partner to locate. Once pupils are confident with locating and describing features on satellite images provide a large-scale OS map of the same area. Ask them to compare their descriptions with symbols for features on the map (and in its key). Were any similar? How did they differ? Could they use the key descriptions to find features in the image?

Teaching activities

Local area stories

Either invite a member of the local community/history group into school to talk about their life in the local area, or source stories from the local library. Encourage your pupils to ask questions, make notes and record information on local maps (e.g. trace the journeys involved) as they listen to/read about where things happened. Groups of pupils could rewrite the story and include maps that follow the action – carrying out checks for accuracy during fieldwork. Even given the same descriptive information, groups will produce different maps, which is a good focus for discussion. (See pages 20-21 for further story ideas.)

Local routes 1: virtually

Identify a place the pupils visit that is near the school (perhaps the local library or park) and explain they are to follow the route virtually. Open Google Maps on the interactive whiteboard and locate your school, then drag the Pegman figure (bottom right) onto the street near your school entrance. (Google Maps will toggle to Google Street View.) Use the mouse to click on the directional arrow along the road (explain that Street View images were captured in a car). As Pegman moves and the next image comes into focus, ask 'what do you see now?' and request directions 'do we go straight on/turn left/right here?' When you reach the destination, ask pupils to draw a map of the route from memory and mark any features they saw virtually. Explain that they will check the route in reality.

Local routes 2: reality

Soon after carrying out the virtual walk, take the class out to follow the same route using their memory maps. Pause to allow pupils to capture digital images along the way and discuss what they see on the ground compared with the virtual walk. Pupils use their digital images to create a real School Street View giving locational and directional information with each image for others to follow the route.

Local street models

Obtain an oversize map of the streets immediately around your school from the Ordnance Survey. Invite pupils to create models of the houses, shops, offices, school and other buildings together with street furniture (e.g. post boxes, traffic lights, litterbins) (see page 13 of Richardson and Richardson, 2016). Pupils place (from memory) their models on the map and label each one. Discuss how they can find out what is missing and whether things are in the right place. They may suggest using satellite images or Google Earth. Explain that they will take digital images of the model out into the local area, and compare the images with the real thing. Display the digital images alongside the model and ask pupils to explain how it evolved.

World wheres

Maps and globes are used to learn about features around the world.

Geographical enquiry and skills

- recognise the relationship between a globe and a world map
- locate key features at different map scales
- enquiry – ask and respond to geographical questions

Geographical knowledge and understanding

- know the globe is a 3D model of Earth
- name world continents and oceans
- identify the Equator, North/South poles, hot/cold regions
- locate and name the British Isles/UK, its capital, constituent parts and surrounding seas/oceans

To access extra resources from the Everyday Guides web page, see page 2.

Photo © Shaun Flannery

The preceding spreads provide a sequence of activities that take primary pupils from the classroom, to the school buildings and grounds, and out into the local environment to build up their locational knowledge and vocabulary. In this spread, pupils use three- and two-dimensional representations of our planet Earth (globes and world maps and atlases respectively) to learn where's where in the world. Working through continental, country and national levels helps pupils become more aware of features of the wider world.

Whatever the focus of your topic, use globes and maps that are appropriate to the age range you teach. Offer pupils opportunities to handle and refer to them. Introduce globes, atlases and world maps with increasing amounts of detail, draw attention to, for example, lines of latitude and longitude in discussing time zones or hot and cold regions of the world. As they compare a globe with maps, pupils can look for features they already know about. Even if they are just slotting the last piece in a map jigsaw, ensure your pupils know where they are in the world.

Questioning a globe

As pupils pass round a softball or inflatable globe that shows a basic map, ask 'What is this?' 'What does it show?' 'How can you tell which bits are land and which are oceans?' Encourage pupils to point out features, e.g. smaller seas/islands, or how colour is used to show higher land. Ask 'What other information could the globe show?' and record their responses.

Teaching activities

Create a globe

Provide small groups with a globe and a sphere (e.g. a large orange or grapefruit balanced on a section of cardboard tube) and copies of the 'Blank continent outlines' (see web page) at a scale appropriate to the spheres. Challenge the groups to create a three-dimensional representation of Earth by finding out the name of each continent and planning where to locate it (e.g. mark the Equator, Prime Meridian and poles on the spheres as guides) before pasting (or drawing) it on their sphere. When their globes are complete with labels, reinforce the pupils' locational knowledge by asking 'Which continents lie north/south/across the Equator?' 'Which are closest to Antarctica?', as well as 'How could you show extra information?'

My world 1

Ask pupils to draw a map of their country or the world from memory. What do they include and why? How many places and features do they include? They compare their map with a national/world map and discuss what they want to learn to improve and develop it. Save their maps digitally to refer back to later.

Images of our country

Establish what a capital city is then ask pupils to name the capitals of the United Kingdom's four nations and locate them on maps of the UK and British Isles. Pairs of pupils use the internet to find out about landmarks in each capital and discuss their findings. Provide a variety of images of rural and urban areas in the UK and ask groups to prepare a presentation on just how varied the UK landscape is.

Where in the world poster

In response to the question 'What does the word "country" mean to you?' some pupils will say 'I live in the country' (meaning the countryside), while others may say 'Brazil is a country'. Ensure pupils recognise they live in 'a country' even when they live in 'the countryside' and that different people live in different countries around the world. Give pairs of pupils a different blank country shape (see web page) and ask them to locate it on a globe, use an atlas to find out two facts about it, write their facts on it then cut it out. Invite pupils to create a 'Where in the world poster' by placing their outlines in the correct location on a world map. Ask 'Will our world poster ever be complete?' and encourage pupils to look out for and add appropriate locational information from the television, radio, social media and the internet.

Storyworlds

Pupils encounter places around the world through stories.

Geographical enquiry and skills

- use globes and atlases to find places
- notice named real places in stories
- enquiry – ask and investigate geographical questions

Geographical knowledge and understanding

- realise that some places in stories are real and others are not
- locate on a globe and world map places in stories
- describe what the stories say about the places they encounter

References

Maldonado, S. and Glynne, A. (2015) *Ali's Story*. London: BBC Learning.

Manning, M. and Granstrom, M. (1998) *Out There Somewhere it's Time to…*. London: Franklin Watts.

Readman, J. and Roberts, L. (2002) *The World Came to My Place Today*. London: Eden Project Books.

Tanner, J. and Whittle, J. (2013) *The Everyday Guide to Primary Geography: Story*. Sheffield: Geographical Association.

To access extra resources from the Everyday Guides web page, see page 2.

Photo © Anna Grandfield

Storybooks are a valuable resource in geography-led topics. Illustrated stories set in real places or in imaginary places in real countries or continents can help extend your pupils' locational knowledge. Use place-based picture books to introduce them to a particular geographical theme (e.g. the impact of climate change on the planet), take your pupils on an enquiry-based journey across continents (e.g. follow a character's migration route), or talk about day and night around the world. As they read, encourage your pupils to refer to a globe, world map or atlas to locate named places; it can enliven the narrative. Where a story offers some information about a place, pupils can use the internet and reference books to discover more.

Where in *Ali's Story*

Before introducing the book, talk about how and why people make journeys from one country to another and record pupils' initial responses. Read, *Ali's Story* (Maldonado and Glynne, 2015), in which Ali tells of his life in Afghanistan and his migration to the UK, where his family eventually settle. Revisit pupils' earlier responses and (if migration was not mentioned) add it to the list as well as the new information that pupils volunteer. Pupils find Afghanistan on a world map. (See pages 30–1 of Tanner and Whittle, 2013, for more on exploring migration.)

Teaching activities

It's time to...

Use stories to introduce the idea of time differences around the world (e.g. Manning and Granstrom, 1998). Encourage pupils who have visited different time zones (perhaps on holiday) to talk about their experiences. Access an online webcam in a city on the other side of the world (see web pages) to show that while it is daytime in the UK it is night there (refer to a globe as you do so, perhaps shining a torch on one side to demonstrate this). Explain that these activities are a precursor to more in-depth work on time zones (see pages 30-31).

Place a story

Challenge pupils (perhaps in pairs) to write their own story based on a journey to real cities, features, countries, seas, and so on. Pupils use the globes, atlases and maps they have produced to locate a starting point, places to pass through and where their story ends. For extra authenticity, pupils could research images of these places via the internet (although you will need to vet the sources). Provide a range of storybooks as stimulation for writing – see web page. Encourage pupils to share their stories with different audiences (e.g. family, friends).

The world of everyday goods

The World Came to my Place Today (Readman and Roberts, 2002) offers insights into the sources of everyday goods and encourages pupils to consider links between themselves and the wider world. Pupils list 5–10 items that their family use or consume everyday (e.g. a favourite food, toy or computer game), then carry out internet research on where each item is made and how it reaches the place they bought it. Create an 'everyday goods' display, showing images of or packaging from the goods linked to a world map with string.

Topically where?

Pupils learn about topical places.

Geographical enquiry and skills

- enquiry – ask and investigate geographical questions
- use maps at different scales
- talk about where places are

Geographical knowledge and understanding

- locate places locally, nationally and globally
- name and locate countries around the world
- know the location of national and world key topographical features

Photo © Chris Northwood

Places are topical. When an event occurs, the news media will name the place(s) and features (streets, village, city, country, sea, environments, etc.) to situate the event in the world. Often the reports include maps, sometimes with a larger-scale map of the place shown alongside a smaller one of the region. This helps pupils to relate where the event has occurred to places they already know of, thus extending their mental maps. Places also become topical, for example, as the settings for the latest television drama series, cinematic film, or a sporting event. The immediacy of topical places can pique pupil interest and provide the motivation for an in-depth geographical study. It is also important for pupils to learn where events took place in the past, because this contributes to their understanding of current events.

What's topical with me

Ask pupils to complete the 'What's topical with me' questionnaire (see web page) to identify places and features they are currently interested in, which are worth investigating. Gather their responses and, as a class, decide which topical places/features to investigate in geography.

To access extra resources from the Everyday Guides web page, see page 2.

Teaching activities

Where in the news

Gather a number of recent national and international newspapers and/or provide access to digital news sources for groups to investigate. Groups search for and list the names of countries, cities, regions, rivers, mountains, and other places/features. They record how many times each place/feature is mentioned, then divide their list by type of place or feature. Groups use atlases to locate these places/features, mark them on national/world maps and look for any patterns. Discuss topicality: why are some places mentioned more than others?

My holiday where

List all the holiday destinations that pupils have visited or know about. Pairs choose one holiday destination to investigate and create a poster that encourages people to visit. They carry out research using a range of resources, including newspapers, atlases, reference books and the internet, to discover where the place is, what it is like and what people can do there. They must include a map and information about how to travel there. Display the posters and invite others (adults and pupils) to add sticky notes saying which place they would most like to visit.

A change of scene

Many television series and cinematic films are recorded in real places around the world and trailers posted online (see, e.g. YouTube, BBC, Channel 4). (You will need to identify a trailer that is appropriate to the age range you teach and vet the content before using it in class.) Show an extract from the trailer to the class once all the way through. Explain that, although many films/television series are works of imagination, the settings are often real places. Show the extract for a second time, pausing to discuss each change of scene and allow small groups of pupils to make notes (e.g. for *Harry Potter* this could include 'Diagon Alley', 'inside a wand shop', 'outside a castle', 'in a big dining hall'). (You can use the settings cog to the bottom right of the screen to turn off the sound and slow the playing speed by half.) Use the time code to divide the extract into short sections and designate a section to each group. Challenge the groups to discover as much as they can about each setting, then write and record a 'voiceover' that gives locational information (with maps and images) about the settings shown in their section of the trailer. If possible, arrange for the groups to present their voiceovers to a wider audience, e.g. other classes, parents/carers.

Discovering where in atlases

Pupils learn to use atlases to explore places and features.

Geographical enquiry and skills

- find places in national and world atlases
- talk about where places are
- enquiry – ask and investigate geographical questions

Geographical knowledge and understanding

- know that there are different types of atlases
- understand the range of information atlases contain
- read symbols, use the contents page and follow directions
- locate countries, cities and physical features

Resources

Times Atlas of the World
Oxford First Atlas
Worldatlas

To access extra resources from the Everyday Guides web page, see page 2.

Photo © Creative Commons Licence

In 1595, Gerardus Mercator published the first collection of maps of the world, nations and regions. Mercator chose to call it an Atlas (after the Greek Titan Atlas) and the term became synonymous with bound collections of maps. Over the years, world atlases developed – and now range from very detailed reference atlases (e.g. *The Times Atlas of the World*) to ones aimed at young children (e.g. *First Atlas*). Atlases that have a specific purpose include road atlases (for navigation) and thematic atlases (on climate or land use). Today's pupils often interact with electronic atlases (e.g. *Worldatlas* – see web page), which contain up-to-date information on places and features around the world. You should ensure that the class collection of atlases is as eclectic as possible, to enable pupils to apply their knowledge of where's where at a range of scales.

What's in an atlas?

Create a 'What's an atlas?' display of atlases with question bubbles attached. Encourage pupils to familiarise themselves or refresh their knowledge of atlases by asking 'what is in an atlas?', 'what does the contents page show?' and 'how helpful is this?'. Working in pairs, pupils refer to the contents page to find specific maps. Pupils can explore why different types of atlases are available. Prompts can include 'what kind of atlas would someone use to choose a holiday destination?' and 'what kind of atlas might a lorry driver use?'. Add these questions to the speech bubbles together with pupil responses.

Teaching activities

Atlas map symbols

Select a particular world atlas map and give pairs of pupils clues about what it shows so they can locate it. Pairs study the map then share what it shows with others. For example, on a country map they could name different cities, rivers and mountains, saying which are near each other. Ask how pairs located the features they mention and discuss which symbols they referred to. Encourage them to notice the different point, line and shape symbols, colours and words; refer to the key. Pupils source images of a particular city, river or mountain (on the internet) to find out what it really looks like. Is this what they expected? Can they devise a more accurate symbol?

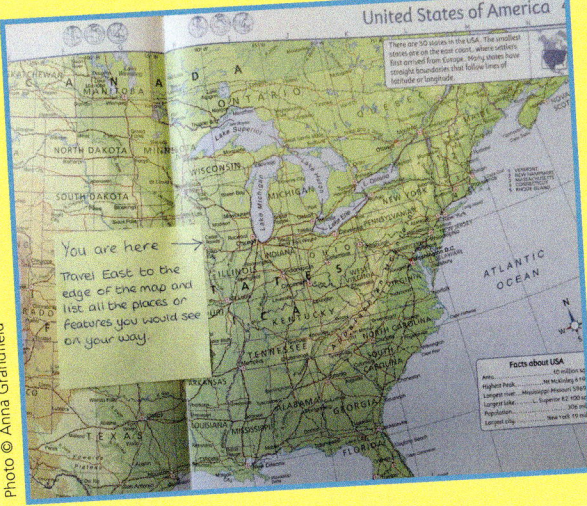

Which direction?

If necessary, refresh the pupils' knowledge of 'north', 'south', 'east' and 'west' using compasses. Choose a place on an atlas map and challenge different pupils to 'travel' north, south, east or west until they reach the edge of the page. They must list all the features or places that lie in that compass direction. (Explain that atlas maps are usually printed so that north is at the top of the page.) When pupils are familiar with the activity, ask pairs to repeat it using different atlas maps. They give another pair the page number from the atlas contents, the starting point and the features/place names along the way. The second pair use the clues to discover the compass direction travelled. Pupils can produce directional travel strips and place them correctly around a compass on a desk or table.

Compare globes with atlas maps

Provide pairs with a globe and an atlas. One pupil gives the name of a continent or ocean on the globe and the other finds the atlas pages that show it. They check the globe against the atlas map then swap resources and do the same for countries and physical features. Discuss when and why it is best to use an atlas map and when a globe. Add a globe to your 'What's in an atlas?' display together with some pupil responses.

How the atlas got its name

Hand out copies of 'How the atlas got its name' (see web page) and provide images of the historical maps it mentions for the pupils to study. They choose and write about one of the historical atlas maps. Alternatively, pupils could compare how the world appeared then to how it appears in a modern atlas map.

Locating places and features

Pupils learn about the role of grid lines on maps.

Geographical enquiry and skills

- locate sites on atlas maps
- use alpha-numeric grid references on maps
- use an atlas index
- use geographical vocabulary

Geographical knowledge and understanding

- understand the significance of latitude and longitude
- main lines of latitude (the Equator, tropics of Cancer and Capricorn, Arctic and Antarctic circles)

To access extra resources from the Everyday Guides web page, see page 2.

Photo © Anna Grandfield

Evenly spaced vertical and horizontal lines that form a grid appear on most types of maps. These grid lines enable us to say precisely where a site is on a map. Some maps have letters from left to right along the top and numbers up the side – forming an alphanumeric grid that pupils can use to identify a grid square and locate, e.g. places listed in an atlas index. Grids on other maps use numbers: the resulting 4- and 6-figure grid references enable us to precisely locate sites within a grid square. On world maps, for the lines of latitude and longitude, degrees (°) are the unit of numbering. Sailors, pilots and others use the lines of latitude and longitude to know precisely where they are as well as to navigate around the world. If maps are visual representations of data (features and places) then it is grid references that allow pupils to pinpoint specific features and places in the world with a great level of accuracy. Almost everything in the world can be located and tracked using grid references – including hand-held electronic devices such as smartphones.

Alphanumeric streets

Provide a group of pupils with a copy of a local A–Z street atlas (see web page) and ask them to use the index to find the roads they each live on. The index lists streets by name and will give an alphanumeric grid reference then the page number (e.g. Solly St – 1D 98) or a similar combination. Pairs can carry out the same activity using a road or national atlas, but giving each other the name of a place to locate.

Teaching activities

Grid references games

Hand out copies of the 'How to read grid references sheet' (see web page), an extract from an Ordnance Survey map at 1:25,000 scale and sets of the map symbol cards (see web page). Allow small groups to familiarise themselves with identifying the OS symbols and giving 4-figure grid references when they locate a symbol on a map. Then challenge the groups to devise a 'Grid references game'. Groups could evaluate each other's games in a play session.

You read the horizontal grid reference from left to right (West to East); these horizontal numbers or letters are called 'Eastings'.

You then read the vertical grid reference from bottom to top (South to North) and these numbers or letters are called 'Northings'.

The grid reference for each square of the grid refers to the southwest corner of that square.

A good mnemonic to remember that you need to read along before up is: You have to go along the corridor before going up in the lift.

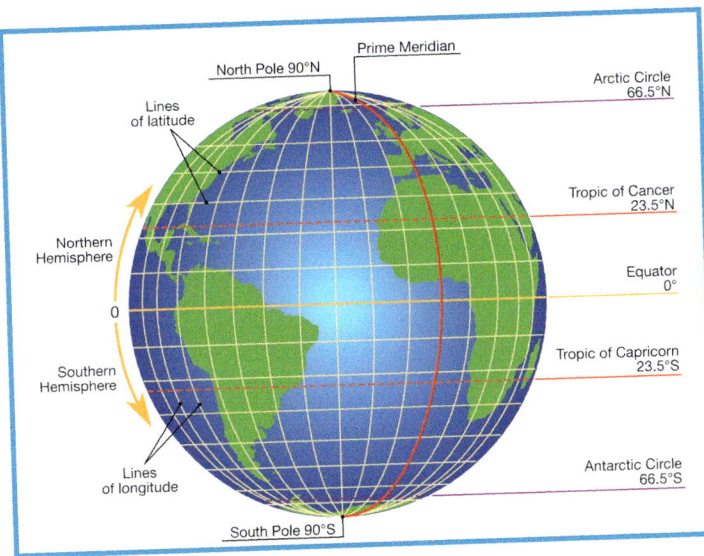

Latitude and longitude

Trace the lines of latitude: the Equator, tropics of Cancer and Capricorn, and Arctic and Antarctic circles; then the Prime Meridian and other longitude lines on a world map. Pupils study the degree numbers at the perimeter of atlas maps for each line of latitude and longitude marked. They follow the numbers north, south, east and west and check the intervals between the numbers on different map scales. Provide copies of the 'Latitude and longitude' information sheet (see web page). Discuss what the numbers indicate, why there may be 10° or 20° degree intervals between them and why some maps do not show every line of latitude or longitude.

Enquiry into latitude and longitude

Groups are to conduct an enquiry into the locational importance of lines of latitude and longitude. Groups devise their own key question on the origins of lines of latitude and longitude and use this to generate sub-questions on why and how the lines have been used over the centuries and by whom. You could say that, during their investigations, groups will encounter pirates, Harrison's chronometer and smartphones. Groups are to share their findings in illustrated presentations.

GPS uses

Discuss how different organisations use co-ordinates generated from latitude and longitude in global positioning systems (GPS) to learn about the behaviour of wildlife (e.g. tracing the seasonal migration of birds), to ensure aeroplanes and ships are on course and even to locate gritter lorries in Scotland. Create a class list and encourage pupils to add to it as they find other instances of GPS use.

My country, my place

Pupils focus on what a country consists of.

Geographical enquiry and skills

- use street, road and national atlases
- locate places/features and gather information about them
- enquiry – ask and investigate geographical questions

Geographical knowledge and understanding

- locate their country in Europe and the world
- know what a country and capital city and major cities are
- locate main human and physical features and regions
- know the countries, islands and seas near the UK

To access extra resources from the Everyday Guides web page, see page 2.

Photo © Anna Grandfield

Pupils' locational knowledge of their country will be based on where they have read or heard about in the media, and from family discussions and travel. Depending on personal experience, pupils' national memory maps may already include the capital and extend to other cities, resorts and features, or focus on places near where the pupil lives. Whatever their starting point, studying their country should involve looking at rural and urban areas, coastlines, ports and seas, so that pupils can appreciate the sheer variety of landscapes in the British Isles/United Kingdom. Investigations into links between their home and other regions will help pupils to make the necessary connections between the different parts and to other countries. During topic work, ensure that your pupils are sufficiently confident in knowing what's where that they can point out examples from their country.

What's in a region?

Explain that when we talk about countries to aid location, we often break them into regions, for example 'the southwest' or 'the Lake District'. Discuss which region your school, neighbourhood, town or city is in and challenge pupils to find out what they can about it. They should consider the origin of its name: does it refer to …the landscape? …its location in the country? …past industrial activity? Ask 'what are the region's other characteristics?'. Pupils can investigate another region and compare it with their own.

Teaching activities

Capital cities

Pupils study a UK map showing cities and towns. Ask 'which cities/towns have you heard of or visited and why?' and record their responses. Draw their attention to how different-sized cities are shown on the map/in the key, including the capital. Ask 'what is significant about a country's capital city?' (usually it is where Parliament, the President/Monarch's palace and other government buildings are located) and invite pupils to investigate the importance of, e.g. London in the UK. Extend the study to capital cities in neighbouring countries and use the handout 'What's in a name?' (see web page) to initiate a discussion about what a city is.

As the crow flies

Using a map of their country, pairs travel 'as the crow flies' (i.e. in a straight line) from one named place to another. For example, using a road atlas map of England, 'go due north from Oxford and record which settlements you pass over on your way to Newcastle upon Tyne'. Alternately, pupils can record what is due north/north-west/east/south-east within 25km, 50km or 100km of a given physical feature. Pairs swap over and start from another city or feature, using a different direction of travel and destination/measurement.

Photo © Helen Clarke

Photo © Paul Daniels

Holiday resorts

Pupils can check local newspapers, hoardings and travel agents' window displays to discover which places in their country are popular as holiday resorts. Pairs choose one resort and investigate where it is and what attracts people to it. They create an advertising poster, leaflet or booklet, which includes maps (showing where it is located) plus information on how get to the resort from their locality. Create a 'Holiday resorts' display.

Pictorial maps

Gather a variety of newspapers, magazines, holiday/tourist brochures, city guides, postcards, etc., of your country. Invite pairs or small groups of pupils to search the resources for physical features (including mountain ranges, river valleys and groups of islands) and human features (cities, roads, railway lines, and so on). Pupils refer to atlases to find where these features are and what they are like. They then create a pictorial map using images/text from the resources. To build on their factual knowledge, ask pupils to label each feature and add symbols and a key to their map.

Exploring time zones

Earth's rotation and time zones are the focus of a series of exciting activities.

Geographical enquiry and skills

- use atlases and globes
- geographical vocabulary
- enquiry – ask and investigate geographical questions

Geographical knowledge and understanding

- understand the significance of longitude and latitude on maps
- know about the Prime Meridian and the International Date Line
- understand how time zones link to day and night

To access extra resources from the Everyday Guides web page, see page 2.

Photo © Dominic Alves

Pupils find the idea of time zones fascinating because they involve travelling backward and forwards in (day) time around Earth. Geography-led work on time zones can involve cross-curricular work with science and maths. The tasks outlined here are designed to equip pupils with the knowledge of how Earth's rotation helped scientists to devise a method for delineating time zones using lines of longitude. Feel free to adapt 'Explaining time zones' to the needs of your pupils.

Explaining time zones

Spin a globe to explain that Earth takes 24 hours (or one day) to rotate 360°, and one hour to rotate 15°. Use atlases to show how this information helped scientists to divide the world into time zones – each generally (there are exceptions!) 15° of longitude apart. A toy bird helps demonstrate how flying west 15° of longitude (say from the Prime Meridian) is normally equal to going back one hour, while travelling east 15° of longitude means going forward one hour. Travel north or south within a time zone and the time will usually stay the same. Lay a ruler vertically on an atlas map to indicate that not all time zones align neatly with lines of longitude. Point out that China, for example, sticks to one time zone across the whole country, but Russia (among others) has several time zones. Shine a torch on the globe to demonstrate that when it is midday at the Prime Meridian, or 0° longitude (which passes through Greenwich in London, UK), it is dark on the other side of the world. Explain that it is in the middle of the Pacific Ocean where the east and west lines of longitude converge at 180° (two 180° protractors laid back to back) – an imaginary line (or International Date Line) where the date changes. This line of longitude is also wonky, so that island countries in the central Pacific Ocean can use the same date. Finally, ask 'how are different time zones helpful?' and use the pupils' responses to start a time zones display.

Teaching activities

Time travellers

Display a world time zones map and recap that the pupils should subtract one hour usually for every 15° they travel west (backwards) from the Prime Meridian, and add one hour for every 15° they travel east (forwards) from it. Pupils use the internet to choose an airport in the UK and a destination that is to the east, west, north or south. They track the flight path, noting any time zone changes. Pupils can check each other's calculations then mark their flights on a whole-class time zones map, indicating how long each one takes.

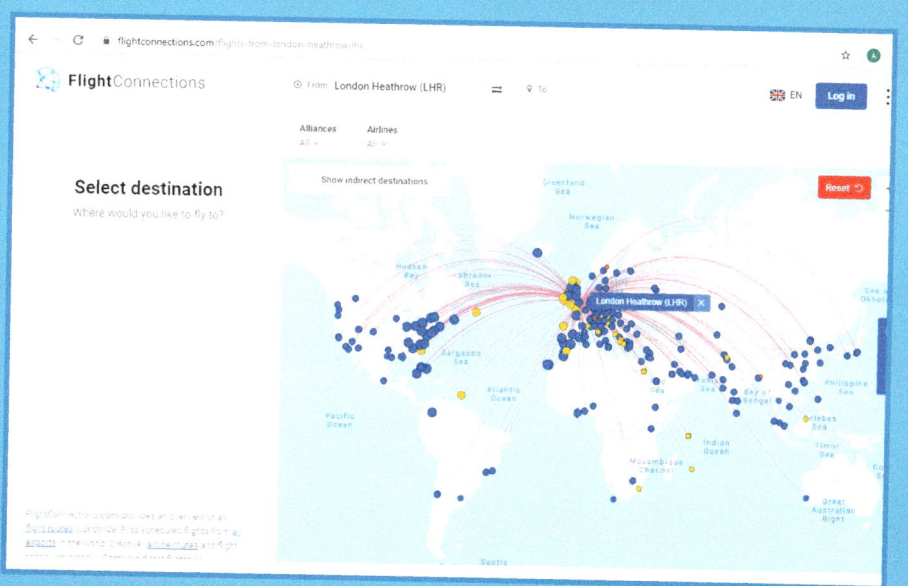

The time here, the time there

Show a web cam in a city on the opposite side of the world. Pupils locate the city on a map. Web cams usually display the time so pupils can compare it with their own time and work out the time difference. Discuss what people may be doing in that city. Repeat the activity with webcams in neighbouring countries and elsewhere in the world. The pupils can add annotated screenshots from different web cams as part of the class time zones display.

> Dear everyone
> This is my last stop on my travels to the International Date Line and I am in Auckland, New Zealand. I have travelled through 12 time zones now, so here it is 8.45 in the morning on Saturday 17 August, which means at home in England it is 8.45 in the evening on Friday 16 August!
> Love Julia xxx
>
> Class Y6SC
> Solly Junior School
> Solly Street
> Sheffield
> S1 4BF
> United Kingdom

Skype/email school links

If your school has links with schools in countries in other time zones, build in an opportunity for the pupils to focus on the time difference between their two schools. During email/Skype communications, pupils could question each other about their day. Your pupils can then use the responses (with permission of the other school) as the basis for speech bubble conversations that can be added to the class time zones display.

The time along the way

Recap or allow pupils to discover for themselves what and where the International Date Line is, why it is called the IDL and why it is not a straight line of longitude. Ask some pupils to plan a journey travelling west from their country, and the others to plan a journey going east. They must all reach the International Date Line. Pupils choose several locations along the way and, as they stop off at each one, they write a postcard home. On each postcard, they must include the time and explain how many time zones they passed through. Pupils could decorate the front of their postcards. Add the postcards to the time zones display and celebrate its completion with the pupils.

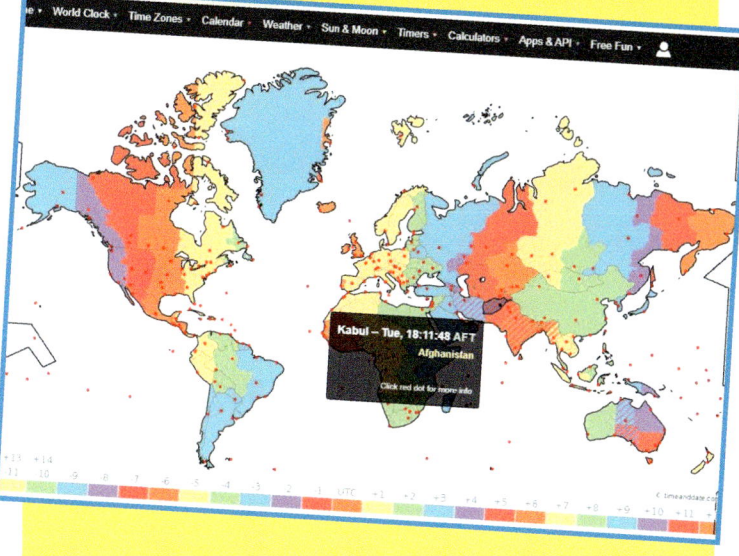

Themes, projections and world regions

Pupils investigate thematic maps, map projections and world regions.

Geographical enquiry and skills

- use map symbols and a key
- use compass directions about the world
- enquiry: asking and investigating geographical questions

Geographical knowledge and understanding

- know about thematic maps and their uses
- know about the world's significant regions and hemispheres
- know maps can be centred differently on the world
- know that there are different world map projections

Photo © Anna Grandfield

There is no single definitive map of the world. Over the centuries cartographers have represented the world in many different ways. As pupils soon discover, the problem is to produce a flat map of our spherical Earth. Mapmakers have tried to overcome the distortion of country shapes by developing different map projections. However, pupils will mostly encounter equal area projections in their school atlases, because this projection aims to show the regions of the world as accurately as possible. Many pupils enjoy studying thematic maps, which present information about the world distribution of volcanoes and earthquakes, populations, biomes, etc. As they do so, they will encounter location-based terms like 'northern hemisphere', 'the West' and 'Middle/Far East' all of which help extend their vocabulary and deepen their knowledge of where's where.

A distorted world

Pupils draw the continents on an orange then peel it; they will soon see that it does not lay flat like a world map. Next, they use their orange peel to draw a map of the world (a form of interrupted projection). Display different map projections (including a Mercator's, an equal area, an interrupted and a Peters) and ask pupils which projection they think is most and which least helpful. They write their reasons on separate sticky notes and place them on the appropriate projections. Which is the most/least preferred?

To access extra resources from the Everyday Guides web page, see page 2.

Teaching Activities

Naming world regions

Hand out copies of the 'What's in a name info sheet' (see web page) and ask pupils to name as many regions of the world as they can in two minutes. Record their responses and divide the list. Encourage different pupils to discover what particular names mean and mark them on a world map. As they encounter other regions, encourage pupils to add them to the map with detail.

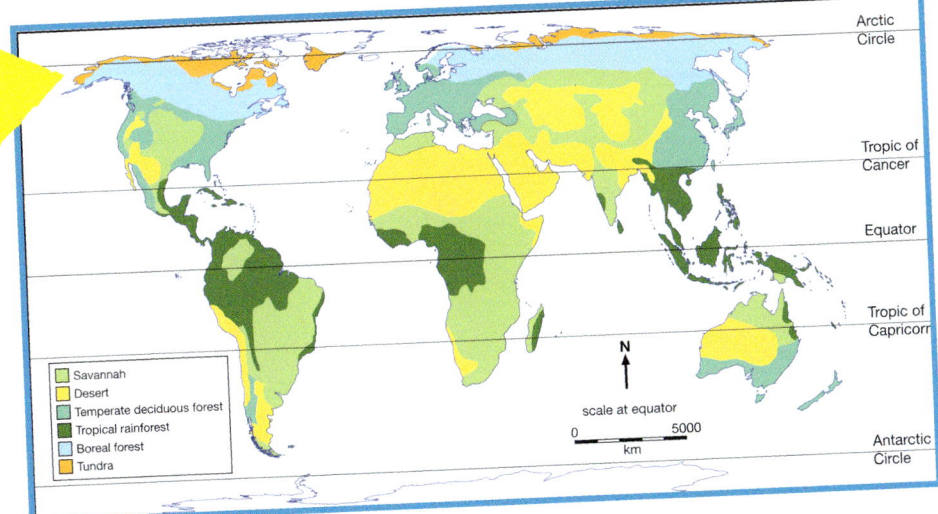

Investigating thematic maps

Using one biome (e.g. tundra) as an example, describe what a biome is. Ask small groups to identify an atlas map that shows biomes and/or environmental regions of the world. First, the groups describe the variety of biomes shown on one continent; then they map the world distribution of one of these biomes; and, finally, they outline why biomes are important for life around the world. Groups present their findings to the rest of the class. (You can adapt this activity for use with different thematic maps.)

Worldmaps.alt

Remind pupils that most world maps are printed with north at the top and are Atlantic-centred, but not all. Provide groups or pairs with an alternative worldview map. These include a map centred on the Pacific Ocean, the Australian 'up-side down' map and North or South polar projections. Groups decide who might use the map and how different people might respond to it. Challenge pupils to decide whether their own mental maps, which have them at the centre, are 'worldmaps.alt'!

Thematic worlds

Groups of pupils create a thematic map based either on their own country, showing the distribution of natural features or out-of-town retail outlets, for example, or on an aspect in the wider world (e.g. a world coffee map). Groups must give reasons for choosing their theme, saying, for example, why particular natural features are important to people, and identify any patterns on their map. As many pupils are familiar with building worlds in electronic or online games, they could use some gaming ideas to present their findings.

Which places should we know?

Photo © Bryan Ledgard

Pupils are able to justify the value of their local to world locational knowledge.

Geographical enquiry and skills

- use globes, atlases and maps, and digital mapping to locate places and provide directions
- justify decisions about place and location choices
- enquiry – ask and investigate geographical questions

Geographical knowledge and understanding

- name and locate the cities and some key physical features and significant places nationally
- locate a number of countries, physical and human features across the world
- appreciate the importance of knowing places and features
- explain the significance of key places and features

To access extra resources from the Everyday Guides web page, see page 2.

Is there a shared world knowledge we all should learn so that there is a commonality in our local, national and global mental maps? Perhaps it would help when we discuss features, places and events around the world. In this final unit on where's where, you can encourage your pupils to think about the places/features they already know about locally. Are the places significant to them? If so, in what ways? If not, why not? Which places in the wider world have their parents/carers introduced them to, and why? Widen the discussion to just how much locational knowledge pupils share with other members of the class. Could it be entirely down to what they have learned in geography? Does the curriculum mean that this is inevitable? This can act as a starting point for raising wider questions concerning where pupils ought to know about nationally and globally and could form the basis for a term or half-term project.

My world 2

Invite pupils to draw a map of their country and/or the world from memory – their mental map. They decide what to include rather than attempt to record everything they know, and must justify their decisions. Encourage them to use symbols and a key, and label places and features. Compare the finished maps with those produced at the start of their work on locational knowledge (see p.19). If you want to know more about memory maps, have a look at the Mapping the City project – see web pages.

Teaching Activities

Where matters in our country?

Pupils list the places and features they know of in their country, locate each one in an atlas and create a map showing each place/feature. Which are the most common places/features on the pupils' maps? Consider possible reasons for this. Which parts of the country do pupils know least about? Agree as a class, which are the 'must know' places.

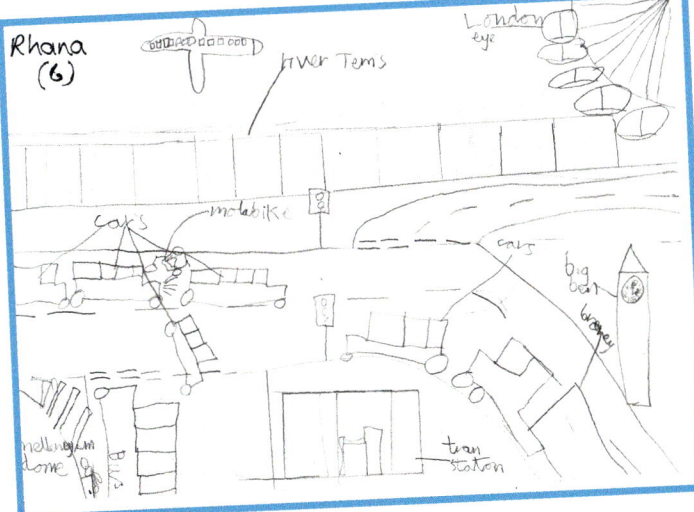

Deciding where: a committee meeting

Organise the room for a committee meeting and explain that the class must compile a list of features and places, which all 11-year-olds must be able to locate on a world map. Provide criteria you have drawn up (or let the pupils devise this), for example, 'It must include physical features, major cities, famous places, countries and capitals, holiday resorts [and so on]'. Guidance could include the number of places/features under the criteria or limit the number of features. Each group must research, present on a map and justify its choices. Hold a whole-class debate and vote on the choices. Pupils can present the final list to the school governors.

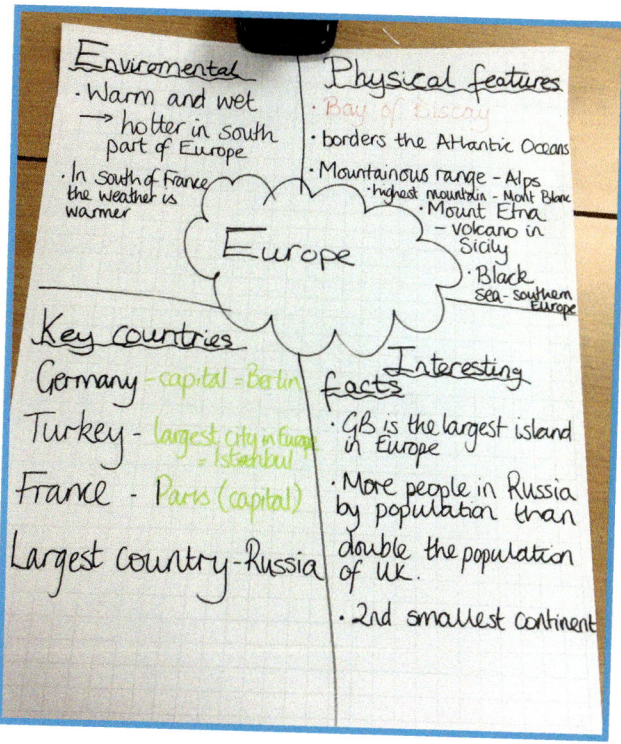

One world recipe

Use a recipe from a cookbook to develop pupils' sense of interdependence with other places. Ask pairs to choose one ingredient from your favourite recipe. They must investigate how and where that ingredient is grown, where it passes through along the route, how it reaches their area, where it is processed and what it is used for. Pairs draw the route their ingredient takes on a whole-class world map and display their findings alongside it. Draw their attention to how food links your country with all parts of the world. Celebrate by holding a 'where's where' taster meal, invite pupils to bring in samples of their favourite food… and enjoy!

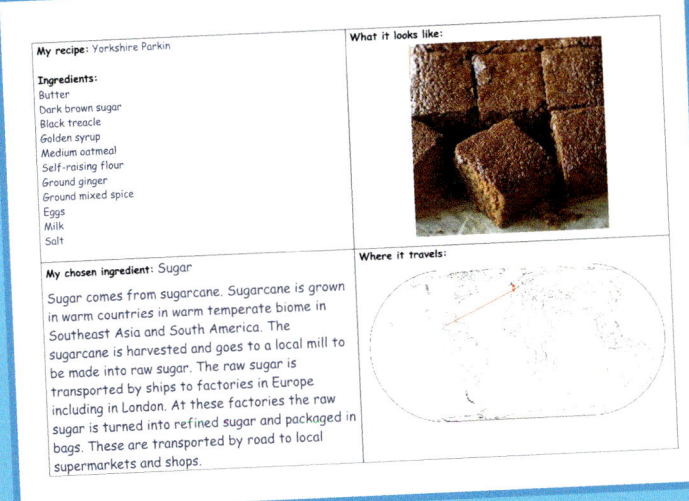

Digitally where?

Pupils find out which places in other continents their family members have digital links with. They list the places and describe each link (for example, 'Edmonton, Canada, … to a cousin, …using Facetime'). Alternatively, pupils could locate the places they know from television and other media, or that family members have visited. Create a digital contacts list similar to those found on social media (use pseudonyms to protect anonymity).

References and further links

References and further reading

Barlow, A. and Whitehouse, S. (2019) *Mastering Primary Geography*. London: Bloomsbury.

Cannons, J. (2020) 'Feedback to feedforward: A teacher's perspective', *Primary Geography*, 101, pp. 14-15.

Catling, S. (2017) 'Mental maps: Learning about places around the world' in Scoffham, S. (ed) *Teaching Geography Creatively* (2nd edition). Abingdon: Routledge, pp. 58–75.

Catling, S. and Willy, T. (2018) *Understanding and Teaching Primary Geography* (2nd edition). London: Sage.

Mackintosh, M. (2018) *In the Know: Grid References and map symbols*. Sheffield: Geographical Association.

Pike, S. (2016) *Learning Primary Geography*. Abingdon: Routledge.

Richardson, P. and Richardson, T. (2016) *Everyday Guide to Primary Geography: Maps*. Sheffield: Geographical Association.

Tanner, J. and Whittle, J. (2015) *Everyday Guide to Primary Geography: Local Fieldwork*. Sheffield: Geographical Association.

Tanner, J. and Whittle, J. (2020) *Everyday Guide to Primary Geography: Maths*. Sheffield: Geographical Association.

Wiegand, P. (2006) *Learning and Teaching with Maps*. Abingdon: Routledge.

Willy, T. (ed) (2019) *Leading Primary Geography*. Sheffield: Geographical Association.

Other useful links

A-Z street maps: www.az.co.uk

Bing Streetside: www.microsoft.com/maps/streetside.aspx

Cassini past and present maps: www.cassinimaps.co.uk/shop/downloads.asp

Collins: https://collins.co.uk/collections/reference-atlases

Digimap for Schools: http://digimapforschools.edina.ac.uk/

Encarta world maps: https://microsoft_encarta.en.downloadastro.com/

Geograph Project: www.geograph.org.uk/

Geographical Association shop: https://www.geography.org.uk/Shop/Product-type/Maps-atlases-and-globes/

Google Earth: https://www.google.com/earth

Google Maps: https://www.google.com/maps

Google Maps Mania (you may prefer to vet the contents before allowing pupils to use this blog): http://googlemapsmania.blogspot.co.uk/

MaxiMap: https://maximap.net

National Geographic mapping: https://www.nationalgeographic.org/education/classroom-resources/mapping/

OS Map Reading Made Easy: https://www.ordnancesurvey.co.uk/documents/resources/map-reading-made-easy.pdf

OS Map Symbols: www.ordnancesurvey.co.uk/education-research/resources/map-symbol-sheets.html

OS MapZone: https://www.ordnancesurvey.co.uk/mapzone/

Oxfam Mapping Our World: https://www.oxfam.org.uk/education/resources/mapping-our-world

Oxford University Press: https://global.oup.com/education/dictionaries/subjects/atlases/?region=uk

Philips: www.mapsonline.co.uk/publishers/philips/pb1369.aspx

Primary Geography: https://www.geography.org.uk/Journals/Primary-Geography

Scribble maps: www.scribblemaps.com/maps

TES Geography Quiz using atlases: https://www.tes.com/teaching-resource/geography-quiz-using-atlases-3006762

3D cities on YouTube: https://www.youtube.com/channel/UCpzBVQrFsXVtNNJMztxtxrg

Worldmapper: www.worldmapper.org